SERVAL SON:
SPOTS AND STRIPES FOREVER

Kris M. Smith

Note to readers:

Some of these stories appear in

"DeForest Kelley Up Close and Personal: A Harvest of Memories from the Fan Who Knew Him Best"

Contents

Foreword & Disclaimer

Rainbow Bridge

Ch 1: Meet Baby Deaken

Ch 2: Gabriel Raccoon Joins the Family

Ch 3: Deaken Breaks His Leg (the first time

Ch 4: Mt. St Helens Eruption: Two Fawns Join the Family

Ch 5: Celebrity Deaken

Ch 6: Deaken Bites the Hand that Feeds Him

Ch 7: California Bound (the first time, Sacramento)

Ch 8: A Kitten for Deaken

Ch 9: Deaken Breaks His Leg (the last time)

Ch 10: Return to Washington

Ch 11: Hooray for Hollywood

Ch 12: Jobless in Hollywood

Ch. 13: The Kelleys Meet Deaken

Ch. 14: Critter-sitting at Shambala

Ch 15: Kelleys to the rescue

Ch 16: Who's Visiting Deaken Today?

Ch 17: Deaken Bites Mom (again)

Ch 18: Natural History Magazine Blessings

Ch 19: Landlord Bails, New Home Search

Ch 20: Condo Floods, Deaken Discovered

Ch 21: Deaken's Final Days, the Kelleys' Helping Ways

Ch 22: Our Hearts DO Go On

Appendix: Serval vocalizations, serval videos, Shambala Preserve website

Other Books by the Same Author

SERVAL SON—SPOTS & STRIPES FOREVER

FOREWORD – and DISCLAIMER

I first learned about serval cats—the "poor man's cheetah" — during one of my courses at Ralph Helfer's Wild Animal Affection Training School in Colton CA in 1977-78. I was assigned to **train** a pygmy goat and to **tame** an adult serval cat named Sneakers.

Training a goat is child's play. They teach themselves to walk on 2x4's while you're still lifting the boards into place! They're naturally curious, naturally playful, and naturally "ascendant." Build it and they will climb!

But…**tame** a serval cat?! YIKES!!! That was a whole different matter—a greater level of difficulty. Mr. Helfer said I'd pass the course if I could get Sneakers just to sit or lie quietly near me without hissing or slapping. He wasn't completely sure I could accomplish this feat, so he set the bar low...

Sneakers had apparently been abused (emotionally if not physically) during his time on earth. And servals look ferocious and lethal when they hiss—which they do a lot, sometimes for reasons no one can discern. When they add slapping and backpedaling or crouching and preparing to spring onto your body, they look even scarier. And Sneakers did that… a lot!

Of course, I didn't know any of this at first; I learned as I went along. All I knew about Sneakers was that he was housed in a wooden barrel inside an enclosure that measured about six or eight feet square. I was supposed to go in there and tame him.

Awrighty, then…

Long story short: Over the course of the next eight weeks persnickety Sneakers segued from being one po'ed putty tat to a purring, head-rubbing critter who fell asleep in my arms as I lay beside him under a tree on test day. Helfer came by, saw the two of us cuddled up like Romeo and Juliet, and smiled, "You pass!"

Was I proud? You bet I was. I woulda burst my buttons had I been wearing any to burst. I had tamed an adult serval cat. I mean, taming an adult feral domestic cat is next to impossible, so this was quite the feat, was it not?

Not so fast. I later learned that servals and cheetahs are the Perry Comos of the cat world: you can tame adults caught right out of the wild. Africans did it for millennia, using them as "coursing hounds" to catch faster prey (dik dik and other larger antelopes), then taking the kill, rewarding the cat with a few mouthfuls, and using the rest for their own purposes.

Probably not even Ralph Helfer knew this. During the course, I also was taught "never ever" to leave a serval cat alone with other critters, because servals were rated among the "wildest" of wild animals and should never be trusted with other creatures. I obeyed this precept until my own serval, Deaken, taught me how utterly nonsensical a notion it was. I denied him other companionship for more than six years that he should have had...but more about that later.

You can't believe everything you read in books—except mine. (I'm a straight arrow.)

My 17 years with Deaken were an eye-opener, a heart-warmer, a trauma-inducer and a cherished relationship I expect never to repeat again. And here comes …

The Disclaimer

I don't believe in exotic or wild animals as pets (especially wild cats, wild dogs and simians) for a lot of reasons. The primary reason is that probably less than one tenth of one percent of the people who get them knows what they're getting into, so both parties suffer grievously. There is usually a traumatic and premature parting of the ways. As Ralph Helfer told us in class, "You are responsible for all you tame."

It isn't like you can change your mind and find your critter a new home and a new life with a reputable, responsible caregiver all that easily. Your charges do bond to you, especially since their first few weeks of life are so vital to establishing a relationship that must last into adulthood; one that is safe, sane and sustainable. And too few people have the proper permits to take over if you falter or fail; those who do are usually filled to the brim with other peoples' cast-offs as well as their own broods. And who is going to watch over your wild one when you go on vacation, fall ill, or in some other way must leave them behind for a time for any one of a dozen legitimate reasons?

I knew what I was getting into. I was trained. I read voraciously. I had experience. I had the permits. And I'd had at least 20 domestic kitties before. I was—and remained—committed to nurturing Deaken's life as he grew, and grew, and grew to knee-high and three feet long from tip of nose to tip of tail. How much different could it be to raise a serval when I had raised so many house cats?

Still, I had no idea. Looking back, it was great discipline. Looking back, it was herculean. Looking back, I smile and feel very blessed, but also extremely lucky that it worked out as well as it did. There were times when it could have gone tragically wrong. I carry the emotional scars of all that. I still have nightmares about trying to move heaven and earth to keep Deaken safe from people and people safe from Deaken. Looking back, it is a miracle that more people weren't hurt… that Deaken himself survived largely unscathed.

So, no… I don't advocate wild animal ownership. Although I expect you to fall madly in love with my serval son as you get to know him better, I want you to pay exquisite attention to what it took to sustain the relationship, what it took to meet requirements, what it took to protect lives and property.

It's not a game. Pet ownership itself is a tremendous responsibility. Wild animal stewardship is a whole other level. It is not for amateurs. It is not for dreamers. It is not for people who expect to have children or to have them around. It is not for people who want to take vacations.

Wild animal stewardship is only for people who will dedicate themselves entirely to the wellbeing of their wards. It's a tall order. You're about to discover how tall.

I hope that in learning about Deaken you'll also learn about why sharing him vicariously with you concerns me a little. I know you will love him. Please just don't love him so much that you decide you simply MUST have one of your own. Becoming a wild one's parent is an overwhelming commitment that no one should take lightly. Not even you.

I know your heart is good and that it's in the right place. Enjoy the ride but don't let this story compel you to take on more than you can commit to wholeheartedly… and legally. If you do it wrong, everyone gets hurt.

Imagine loving like this and losing your pet to the authorities because you weren't properly licensed or because your furry darling grievously injured someone. It happens all the time. Lawsuits accrue. Next door neighbors panic.

How quickly everything can change from idyllic to catastrophic.

Few stories end up the way Deaken's and mine did. Remember this as you go along, and I will feel satisfied that you're receiving the whole story, not just the heart-warming parts.

You **are** responsible for all you tame. Don't do it unless you can honor and truly treasure the obligation from Day One to the day your charge crosses Rainbow Bridge.

RAINBOW BRIDGE

When an animal dies that has been especially close to someone here, that pet goes to Rainbow Bridge. There are meadows and hills for all of our special friends so they can run and play together.

There is plenty of food, water and sunshine, and our friends are warm and comfortable.

All the animals who had been ill and old are restored to health and vigor. Those who were hurt or maimed are made whole and strong again, just as we remember them in our dreams of days and times gone by. The animals are happy and content, except for one small thing: they each miss someone very special to them, someone who had to be left behind.

They all run and play together, but the day comes when one suddenly stops and looks into the distance. His bright eyes are intent. His eager body quivers. Suddenly he begins to run from the group, flying over the green grass, his legs carrying him faster and faster.

You have been spotted, and when you and your special friend finally meet, you cling together in joyous reunion, never to be parted again. The happy kisses rain upon your face; your hands again caress the beloved head, and you look once more into the trusting eyes of your pet, so long gone from your life but never absent from your heart.

Then you cross Rainbow Bridge together....

Author Unknown

Chapter One

Baby Deaken

In Yelm, Washington at approximately noon on May 16, 1979, while I was walking Dreyfuss (a leopard/jaguar hybrid) on a leash outside a TV station in Tacoma, desperately trying to convince him to take a leap of faith and step over several large cables which he interpreted as enormous, leopard-eating snakes, Rhodesia Serval gave birth to two small kittens, a male and a female. Her handsome mate, Kenya, had arrived from his namesake country in Africa some years earlier and was hanging out until their kittens' natal day in an adjacent enclosure.

Because Rhodesia (nicknamed Dea) had eaten two previous litters of kittens, we had been on Red Alert to be sure and take the kittens as soon as she delivered them, but we weren't home to do it. Luckily, when we got back at around 4:30, the kittens were still safe. We heard tweets and chirps emanating from the den box and peeked in. There they were.

The sanctuary owner stepped inside and confiscated the newborns. Dea didn't seem to mind. (Nature has a way of informing new parents in the cat family about the viability of their wee ones. Rhodesia's consumption of her earlier litters had been her vote that they could not survive long, and because her own body craved the additional nutrition, she had disposed of them wisely while boosting her own viability.)

For the next several days there were 'round the clock feedings every few hours, resulting in sleepless nights. On the fifth day, the kittens were deemed robust enough for adoption. Because I had been volunteering at the sanctuary for almost a year by this time and had a background in wild animal care, plus the ability to get a Fish and Game permit (since I had been rehabilitating critters for them off and on for years), the sanctuary owner offered me the male. The female was already spoken for.

I chose the name Deaken to honor his origins: Dea from his mom's nickname, and Ken from Kenya, the first part of his dad's name and his dad's place of origin.

Because I was living on my parents' property (although in my own abode), I had talked the matter over with them beforehand. Both were initially vociferously opposed. Finally, I had told them I would move, then, and carry on from some other address. They repented. But Dad told me, "I don't want to see the cat, I don't want to hear about the cat. I don't want anything to do with the cat."

I said, "Fair enough."

(Dad's edict didn't last long. Within weeks, he was lying in bed "finger wrestling" with his spotted "grandson." I didn't bother reminding him that this scenario was not what he had in mind…at all!)

On Day Five of Deaken's new life on earth, I brought him home. He weighed about a pound and fit mostly into the palm of my hand. His eyes were closed, his ears clamped tight atop his forehead. He was grey all over except for his spots and stripes and a few white spots on his muzzle, chin and tummy.

He slept a lot and drank KMR a lot. During his initial vet check, my vet told me he was severely compromised physically; that he had been born with almost paper-thin bones and that I should put him on a proper diet the moment I could start introducing meat to him.

As he slept, I wrote letters to the largest zoos in the country that had servals, telling them Deaken's tale and seeking their advice about his nutritional requirements. Two of them responded almost immediately with identical information: get Zupreem, a Nebraska Brands combination of various meats, grains, vegetables and other body parts created especially for zoo carnivores. I called my vet and asked him to order me two cases.

Sad aside: because Deaken's sister remained on less-nutritious fare as prescribed by the sanctuary owner (who said I was "spoiling" Deaken), she eventually had to be put down because her bones grew so brittle that they would break while she was lying asleep just breathing. It was the research I did that helped Deaken survive and eventually thrive despite his precarious beginning.

As he slowly matured from infant to "toddler" stage, his senses began to kick in. It was remarkable to see. When I brought him home, holding him tight, he had identified me by my scent. He would hiss if someone else picked him up and purr or chirp when I did.

At some point, he began to interpret the world through a new sense. I believe the second sense to kick in was hearing. The moment his ears unfolded and stood up, I was immediately suspect the first time I encountered him from a distance. He heard me approaching, hissed because he hadn't yet learned my walking pattern, and then chirped and ran to me as soon as I was close enough for him to catch my scent. I couldn't help but laugh at his initial confusion, followed by the shock of his recognition.

Not long after his ears opened up his sight cleared, and I immediately became suspect again. He spotted me at a distance that first time, hissed, then heard my footsteps, and chirped and danced in my direction. I just laughed and shook my head. It was remarkable to witness the first use of his developing senses. I will never forget it – although by now I have quite forgotten which sense came second and third to him (after his sense of smell). I think I have conveyed it properly here, but it may have been the other way around. At any rate, it was a series of three separate and distinct occasions.

Chapter Two
Gabriel Raccoon Joins the Family

When Deaken was about six or eight weeks old, a neighborhood boy brought me a box with a baby raccoon inside and asked me to see what I could do to save it. He said he had found it abandoned two days earlier and that, despite all his efforts, it had refused to eat and was slowly starving to death.

I took the little guy and tried to get him to eat. No go. But that evening while I was sleeping in the same room with him (by now he was in a 5' tall, wrought iron bird cage in the living room), I heard him chirr. Listening longer, I heard him again. I sat up and chirred back. Instantly, he came to the side of the cage where I was and chirred again, reaching out with his little paws. I got up, went over to the cage and opened it. He climbed into my arms. I chirred again and offered him a bottle and some food. He ate voraciously.

From that moment on, he became my shadow.

When I introduced the two babies, they adopted each other immediately, without hesitation. Deaken tried to chirr in raccoon and the baby raccoon, who I named Gabriel, tried to chirp in serval. Neither got it exactly right but they didn't care that their new buddy had a slight accent or speech impediment. All was well and good.

By the time September of 1980 rolled around, Gabriel was a teenager in 'coon years, running around outside, strutting his stuff. I had taught him to look in creeks and turn over rocks to find crayfish and other delicacies, and he had taught himself to raid the garbage can, the garden, and anything else he could get into for other cherished goodies. He was particularly fond of two-liter bottles of water or soda: he would roll over onto his back, hold a bottle between all four legs and swig from its mouth like a drunken sailor, then he'd run under the porch with the bottle (and sometimes with tools and utensils, if we left them in harm's way) and taunt us from there to try to come and get him.

Deaken's best fun as a kitten was wading in the shallow pond that lay about fifty feet from Mom's and Dad's chalet. He would go out there and watch for frogs, diving in quickly whenever he saw one. I never saw him catch one, but he never stopped trying.

From infancy, I bathed Deaken frequently (at first) so he would get used to it. I knew that when he was full size introducing him to necessary baths might be problematic, so I started young. I always made it Fun Time. I would fill the tub about knee high (to him) with warm water and then drop in a washcloth. I'd take the tip of the washcloth and drag it through the water to simulate a swimming fish. Deaken would glom onto it as though it was magnetic. He'd even put his face underwater to try and "catch" it. It was always hysterical.

Chapter Three
Deaken
Breaks His Leg

Because of his diagnosed "weak bones syndrome," the first few months of Deaken's life was a race against time. I was feeding him ZuPreem by the time he was six weeks old. His bone x-rays were showing measurable progress, but the vet warned me to keep him as sedate and low-key as possible so he wouldn't fracture anything vital before his skeletal structure improved and carried him out of the danger zone.

I did the best I could, short of caging him in a box for his entire kitten-hood. He would walk, run, roll and race with Gabriel safely enough. (They were so little they weren't able to crunch each other.)

But I made one mistake that I regret to this day. I allowed Deaken to ride beside me on the car seat as I drove around. This was because I recognized how vital it was, these first few months of his life, to expose him to "life in a human's world" so that nothing we crazy people did would ever throw him for a loop and cause him to become anxious.

I took him to work at the sanctuary, took him to the gas station, took him through drive through fast food places. All well and good. He grew up thinking that whatever I did was just fine—all part of his "serval Mom's world."

But one morning I was driving to the sanctuary when he jumped to the floorboard of the car. I slowed the vehicle and called to him to get back on the car seat. He chirped, took a few steps in my direction—winding up between my legs just in front of the driver's seat—and jumped up toward my lap, catching his right rear leg in the steering wheel between the metal-rimmed horn mechanism and the steering wheel.

At the same instant I was approaching a curve in the road, so I snatched him quickly out of the middle of the steering wheel so I could follow the road, not realizing that his foot had become wedged. I heard nothing and he apparently felt nothing because he didn't react at all, but his femur snapped. When I put him down, he didn't try to move again. It was just a short time later that I realized he had been injured.

I rushed him to the vet. Dr. Max asked me how it happened. I was so ashamed that I lied; told him he had been playing and pushed up against the wall with his leg and it broke. He examined it, shook his head, and asked again, "Are you sure that's how it happened? There was no trauma involved?" Since I hadn't heard the bone snap and Deaken hadn't reacted to the break at all, I said, "No. It was just spontaneous."

He said, "That's good. The growth plate probably hasn't been damaged then, so it should continue to grow just fine." I swallowed. And prayed.

Dr. Max said, "His bones are still so thin that there is nothing to pin, so we'll just wrap it and cast it in place. That should work."

Deaken was in a cast for more than four weeks, because Dr Max went on vacation and his associate didn't want to mess with rewrapping Deke's leg. (His associate seemed scared to death of the little guy just because he had spots and stripes. You can see in the photo how little he still was—hardly a threat!)

Deaken's leg grew significantly in length while the cast was on. When it finally came off, Dr. Max noted that Deke's leg had become hyper-extended inside the cast. ("Hyper-extended" is what your cat's leg looks like when it's licking its fur along its stomach or hind end with one leg sticking straight up in the air.) He said, "He's going to need significant physical therapy to get that leg to relax." He showed me how to do it, but the action hurt Deaken so badly that I wasn't able to do it. It made me physically ill even to consider hurting him to that degree. So, in that regard, I failed him. Max said it wasn't a big deal; he could still use the to walk on, stand on his rear legs, and scratch behind his ears.

But it was a big deal. Having a leg that stuck out like a sore thumb left it vulnerable to frequent injury. Eventually he would injure it so seriously that it would have to come off. But before that day arrived, I got on the phone again to exotic vets and took him to a few of them to see what they might suggest, short of physical therapy that was agonizing for him.

One lady vet asked my permission to take Deke to the Woodland Park Zoo and get an opinion from there. I readily agreed.

When they got back, she had a plan. "We're going to put out an APB to all the zoos looking for a donor serval. If one dies, we'll be notified, and we can take a healthy femur from it and replace Deaken's messed up one with that."

I was exultant! I felt it wouldn't be long before a minor surgery could restore Deaken to full viability in his right rear limb.

It was a terrific plan, but no serval donor ever appeared.

Chapter Four

Mt. St Helens Eruption

Fawns Join the Family

Deaken continued to grow and thrive. His bones eventually recovered completely, so his daily routine was expanded. I would let him outside to play in the pond, bob for frogs and salamanders, and carouse with Gabriel—that is, until Gabriel finally heard the call of the wild in late autumn 1980 and took off into adjacent forested areas looking for a mate. It was sad to see him go, but it had been my intention all along to allow him to return to the wild when he felt it was his time.

I've had to let a number of rescued and rehabilitated wildlife (fawns, hawks, skunks, etc.) take the same perilous walk toward whatever destinies awaited them as wild ones. It's never easy because I know the trials and travails that await them out there where not every creature they come across is as benevolent as I am toward them, including other humans. But it's where they belong, and I can't deny them their desire to give their birthright a whirl.

Deaken loved kids and kids loved Deaken. Children up to ages five or so had absolutely no fear of him so they never triggered his fight or flight response. Guileless adults like Carolyn Kelley also were completely safe around him. It was hesitant, fearful older children and adults who set off Deaken's fight or flight response. If anyone approached him who was in the least bit nervous because of their proximity to him, he could feel their anxiety and wanted no part of the interaction. He would growl, hiss, backpedal and slap with his forepaw—which, understandably, didn't make them feel any better about meeting him! Deaken's B.S. detector ("Sure, yes, of course I want to meet Deaken!") was perfect. I got pretty good at detecting the pretenders, too. They were the ones who would reach out to Deaken while leaning as far backward as they could without losing their balance and falling over. I finally learned to tell them, "You're not ready. It's nothing personal. He just knows you're nervous, and that sets off his fight or flight response. He figures if you're approaching him while scared, you must be ready to engage him in a fight… so he responds that way. Make sense?" "No. Yeah, I guess."

When it came to domestic cats and Deaken, I was operating under the preconceived notion—taught to me at Helfer's Wild Animal Affection Training School—that Deaken should never, ever be allowed free rein with other animals, so I always kept him on a leash around them and more than an arm's length away unless a cat approached him and rubbed up against him. When they did, he was always amenable and would chirp at them, but I still clung tightly to the notion that it would be foolish to allow them to actually co-habit with him, no-holds barred. That changed when we moved to Sacramento, but that wouldn't happen for another year yet.

On May 18, 1980 Mt. St Helens—about sixty miles away from us as the crow flies—erupted with such unexpected ferocity that boats in harbors and along the Pacific Ocean 80 miles away jumped off the water. Deaken and I were camping at Ocean Shores when it happened. I didn't know anything had happened, but Deaken did. He sat bolt upright and got very, very nervous.

Soon the camping area was abuzz with the news, and people started packing up and heading for home, since no one was sure where the enormous ash plume might end up as it settled to the ground.

As I drove in the direction of home— which also happened to be in the direction of Mt St Helens—Deaken went nuts. Normally docile when on trips, he rubbed repeatedly against the bars of his enclosure in the rear section of my vehicle, causing a bald and slightly bloodied spot to appear by the time we got home. It was obvious that he knew something huge had happened, and he wanted no part of it.

A few weeks later Fish & Game called me and asked if I was available to bottle feed and nurture two fawns whose mother had perished in the eruption. I quickly agreed, turning Deaken's outdoor enclosure (which he accessed through my bedroom window) into a fawn nursery.

I named the fawns Harry and Jerry (the first one after Harry Truman, the ancient Spirit Lake Lodge owner who refused to leave the area when forewarned of the impending eruption; his 15 cats perished with him; the second one Jerry because it rhymed with Harry. I later found out that Jerry was a Jennifer; the vet had told me I had two bucks; he hadn't looked closely enough).

I securely blocked (I thought) the swinging wooden door between the bedroom and the deer pen to keep Deaken from getting back into "his" pen then spent the first afternoon bottle-feeding the fawns while Deke watched through the window. He looked curious but in no way predatory.

I walked to Mom's and Dad's place for something. When I got back and rounded the corner to the deer pen, I was horrified to find young Deaken's small jaws clamped firmly around one of the fawn's noses. Deke's paws were holding onto the terrified fawn's ears for dear life and he was kicking furiously with his single operable back leg, trying to "disembowel" the poor little ungulate!

I shouted, "Deaken! NO!" as I bolted through the door of the pen. He had no intention of letting go; as far as he was concerned, *this* Bambi was *his*!

I pried Deaken loose and checked out the fawn. It was none the worse for wear, thank God!

It was moments like these that impaled me with the thought that I might be in over my head with this wild cat. As sweet and as loving as he could be, there were times when I realized he was all cat, all wild cat, pure instinct.

I also had an Amazon parrot that I had been given by my vet. It had an inoperable bad eye and its owners had asked Max to put it down because they didn't want a "flawed" parrot. He asked their permission to find it a good home, and they agreed. So I got it.

The bird was a nervous wreck when it arrived. In just three days it was as tame, funny and delightful as they come. It eventually spoke three foreign languages (cat, dog and human) and did the craziest stunts I have ever seen a parrot do. No one taught these antics to it; it just invented them itself.

One day I got home from being out and about and there sat Deaken on my waterbed with the Amazon parrot between his paws, licking it. The parrot was shrieking and ducking; Deaken was just being a daddy cat. He had no intention of hurting the bird, or he would have. It would have been a breeze.

During this time, I ran across a vinyl record that had animal sounds of Africa on it. Thinking it would be a nice present for Deaken, I put it on the record player one day as I cleaned the house.

The first track came on. Birds. Deaken didn't seem to notice much. The second track came on: Monkeys. Deaken was non-plussed. The third track came on. Deaken lowered his head and body and frantically began running around the perimeter of the room, looking for a way OUT. By the time he looked up at the window, considering whether he could jump that high, I had reached the record player and taken the needle from the record. I looked at the label to find out what it was that had made him so anxious. The third track read "Stalking Leopard."

I was astounded.

I wondered, "How does a serval cat who has never been to Africa know what a stalking leopard sounds like?" He hadn't seen or smelled a stalking leopard in our home, or anywhere else in his entire life. How could he KNOW what a stalking leopard would sound like?

It was this experience that convinces me that genetic memory is very real. It's no longer just a theory to me. Later, on another occasion in which actor DeForest Kelley played a part, Deaken would surprise me again in this amazing way.

Chapter Five

Celebrity Deaken

Deaken quickly became a celebrity of sorts in the Pacific Northwest. For as long as he enjoyed it, I would take him around to schools, county fairs and here and there a TV station to introduce him to children and talk about endangered species. I knew that by meeting an endangered species, it would bring home to children the importance of thinking about other creatures who share the planet, too.

At the Western Washington State Fair in Puyallup one year Deaken and I found ourselves in the Natural Resources Building sandwiched between hunters, trappers and fishermen. I wasn't overjoyed with the arrangement, but it was perhaps God's way of forcing me into the strange recognition that people who love the outdoors come in all flavors and proclivities, and during the time I was there I think I made a few converts, while their efforts to convert me were less successful.

One of the celebrities in the same building was Cascade Jack, a TV symbol of the ecology movement. Dressed in deer hide and fur skin cap, he looked like a trapper from the 1860's: big, burly, rugged, calloused.

We eyed each other for the better part of the first afternoon and then he wandered over. Deaken sat in my lap looking lovely, as sweet and tame as could be. I looked up at Cascade Jack and said, "Hello."

He said, "Who's that you have there?"

I said, "His name is Deaken. A serval. Do you want to hold him? He won't bite."

He said, "Sure."

I handed Deaken to Cascade Jack and took their picture. I knew it would turn out great.

He asked if I would send him a copy and I said, "Sure. You can even use it in publicity, if you want."

"Really?"

"Sure. Why not?'

"Thanks. I'll check into that." He gave me his address.

The Humane Society was aware of my public outreach and highly recommended that I have Deaken declawed to limit my liability, especially since I was visiting schools. I thought that was a strange thing for the Humane Society to be recommending, but it made sense, in this case. Although I hated to do it, I did have it done. Amazingly, Deaken didn't even seem to notice. The moment I unwrapped his bandages on the second day, he jumped down from the bed and never even bothered to look at his toes or lick them. His double paw pads must have kept him from experiencing what so many declawed domestic cats go through.

One thing about Deaken that never ceased to amaze me was how fast he could flash his front paws when he was irritated or playing. Over time, I got as fast as he was when we played "catch paws," but it took some doing. His paws moved so fast they were impossible to follow with the eyes—they were a blur. Less than a blur.

Dad grew anxious whenever he watched Deaken and me wrestling. I was always careful to de-escalate any rough-housing that we engaged in, though, if it started to get too intense because I knew how strong Deke was (a 30 pound cat has the strength of a 150 pound muscle man) but I never worried much about him going over the top. We understood each other perfectly. He never tried to out-rank me. We were equals, equals who respected and loved each other.

One time, when Deaken was at this age, he and I were wrestling boisterously in my living room at least sixteen feet across the room from a wood stove. Deaken suddenly stopped playing when something behind the wood stove, hidden completely from view, attracted his attention.

He got up, chirped a little greeting or exclamation. I thought perhaps he had heard Ivanhoe, my German shepherd, walking around on gravel outside the building, but he went directly behind the stove to investigate and started chirping even more excitedly, pawing at his discovery.

Thinking he had perhaps discovered an errant mouse, I went over to investigate and to remove the little critter before it came to grief.

But when I got there and saw Deke's "prey" I was utterly amazed to find that he had heard and responded to an ANT that was walking on the brick floor behind the stove!

Flabbergasted, the next day I wrote to Carolyn and DeForest Kelley detailing Deaken's amazing feat: "I knew servals had good ears, since the encyclopedia says they can hear rodents burrowing three feet underground, but GOOD GRIEF! Can you BELIEVE
this?! I sure wouldn't if I hadn't seen it myself!"

Apparently, De found it impossible to believe. Several years later, he drew a sketch indicating what *he* had decided Deaken had heard lurking outside my cabin in the Pacific Northwest: an elephant eating out of Ivanhoe's dog dish! (You can see De's sketch in my book, ***DeForest Kelley: A Harvest of Memories***, available at Authorhouse.com and at Amazon and other online bookstores.) I just about fell out of the chair laughing! He never missed an opportunity thereafter to jibe

me for making up ridiculous stories about
my marvelous cat!

Chapter Six
Deaken Bites the Hand that Feeds Him

Deaken only bit people three times in his life, always for completely legitimate reasons. Twice, he bit Mom. Once, he bit me.

He bit me while a veterinarian was giving him a vitamin shot in his hip. The vet told me, "Hold onto him tight, because this will sting."

I didn't.

I had Deaken sandwiched between my legs (I was standing up); I was holding his head (lightly, not tightly). As the liquid entered him, Deaken pulled his head out from between my hands, swung it around and bit down, hard, as close to the source of the pain as he could—which happened to be the calf of my leg.

It was a clean entry point. It didn't hurt at all (until the next day, and then it didn't hurt much.) I was amazed; I had always reckoned that a knee-high cat's bite would be more than unpleasant and had hoped I would never find out.

The amazing thing is this: as soon as Deaken realized what he had done, he prostrated himself on the linoleum floor and tucked his head, looking abjectly ashamed. The vet asked me, "Are you all right?" I said, "I'm fine, but look! *He's* miserable!" The vet laughed and shook his head.

The first time he bit Mom was predictable and logical, too. He had chewed a dense rubber ball into little pieces and ingested them, then developed a tummy ache. I noticed that he wasn't acting quite like himself, but he didn't seem sick, either. So I went off to work. But the "something's not quite right with Deaken" idea continued to plague me. (Wild cats will hide their maladies until they become downright urgent because in the wild, an ailing cat quickly becomes a snack for some other predator.) At about 10 a.m., I called Mom and asked her to go over to my place and offer Deaken some cooked hamburger and to report back to me if he didn't eat it. I said, "He if won't eat it, I'll come home and take him to the vet."

Mom went over. Deaken was lying near the front door. She came in, shut the door, and placed a plate of hamburger in front of him. He sniffed it, salivated a little, but didn't take a bite. She could tell he kinda wanted to, but wouldn't.

Sufficiently convinced that something was indeed wrong with Deaken, she stood up and started back out the door but, in doing so, she passed too near the plate of hamburger. He lunged upward and bit her on the leg—not seriously, just a glancing blow—warning her away from the meal he so desperately wanted but didn't feel well enough to eat.

She had innocently violated one of the strictest laws when working around wild animals: you don't put food in front of them and then approach it again. They will go into defensive mode every time.

Mom called to let me know Deaken needed to go to the vet. She didn't even mention that he'd bitten her until I got home, but by then she had figured him out and told me, "I think he thought I was going to take the hamburger away."

One surgery later, I had a handful of rubber as a souvenir and the vet's instructions: It's time to take away from him anything he can chew up.

Deaken would bite Mom one more time, in Encino CA in 1991. More about that later.

Chapter Seven

California Bound (the first time)

In 1980 I began part-time (more or less "on call") as Pacific Northwest Field Services Representative for the Animal Protection Institute, a Sacramento-based animal welfare organization. I quickly got busy helping relocate orphaned grizzly bear cubs from British Columbia Canada (where grizzlies aren't endangered) to Yellowstone Park (where they are) and other pursuits. My knowledge of wildlife and other animal welfare matters was quickly recognized and in February 1981 I was asked to move to Sacramento to join them in the main office so I could help API members all over the nation. At that time I became Field Services Director and Executive Director of Humane Educator's Council, the law enforcement branch of API. (Oh, joy. Damn it, Jim, I'm a teacher, not a policeman!)

But before I could come to California I had to get permission from Fish and Game in the Golden State to allow me to bring Deaken along. I told API it was a deal breaker if I couldn't bring my serval with me.

California doesn't allow wild cats as pets. Period. Getting around this policy was not going to be easy.

I did some research. "For what reasons are wild cats allowed into California?" Results: Entertainment (circus acts, TV shows, etc.), Education (zoos, veterinary schools, etc.), and Research (behavior, medical and other).

Hmmm. OK. Deaken had been in several TV shows already (Lorne Greene's Last of the Wild, PSAs, etc), both for entertainment and for education. So I wrote up a list of his television and live appearance credits, got Creative Services Director Ted Crail to say they'd be using him in an upcoming educational program they would be producing, and submitted it.

One day, though, while I was away from home the phone rang. Mom answered it. It was California Fish and Game. They asked her, "Is the serval a pet?" Mom responded, "Oh, yes. He's a pet. Very friendly." Thinking, of course, that they were inquiring about his character!

When I got home, she told me they had called. I asked, "What for?" She said, "They wanted to know if he was a pet." I got this sinking feeling.

"And you said ---- ???"

"I said of course he's a pet."

"Oh, no…."

"What's wrong?"

"I need to call them back."

"Why?"

"Pets aren't allowed in California."

"What?! Why not?"

"They don't allow people to have wild animals as pets."

I called Fish and Game back and explained the discrepancy: "My Mom was trying to let you know the serval is tame and friendly, that he's not a threat, when she told you he was a pet. He's not strictly a pet. He's an educational tool."

Fortunately, they understood and I was given the go-ahead to move to Sacramento after they made me swear I would never bring in any other wild animals or any additional servals. I agreed.

Of course, when I got there I had to jump through several more hoops and live up to many more rules and regulations than had been required of me in Washington state. Now I had not just Fish and Game as overseers and inspectors, but Endangered Species federal inspectors and city inspectors.

I had to erect an approved facility, fill out dozens of pages of paperwork, pay for numerous inspections, have Deaken "vetted" by an exotic or zoo vet annually on premises and at their clinics because he was an endangered species (or at least, the Barbary Serval was and no one knew what kind of serval he was, so they had to err on the side of the most protection).

The move ended up costing me thousands of dollars over the next 15 years not to mention lots of headaches and angst. But I easily passed every inspection; in fact, at one point an inspector asked me if I would be willing to take in other servals or small cats that they confiscated from illegal owners! I could barely afford the one I had—and hadn't they made me swear not to add to my menagerie before they would even allow us to come into the state? It was confusing, to say the least!

The first time I was inspected in Sacramento I was floored by the agent's lack of knowledge. He was going down the list checking off things, but when he handed me the document to sign, I noticed he had left the "pelage" field blank . I asked him, "Why didn't you rate his pelage?" He looked at it and said, "Oh, I've been meaning to look that one up, but I keep forgetting. I don't know what pelage is." I said, "It means the condition of his coat, the condition of his fur—healthy or unhealthy." "Oh! Thanks!" So he marked his *first-ever* entry in that column. I wondered why he had never been called on it before; figured he must be brand new. So I asked him, "How long have you been an inspector?"

"Five years."

Five years… (???!!!) And no one at his headquarters had asked him why the most telling aspect of an animal's physical wellbeing—the condition of its coat—had never been marked? And he had never looked it up…. In five years??? This was utterly unfathomable to me, ludicrous.

No wonder I had a headache!

Chapter Eight

A Kitten for Deaken

Not long after I got Deaken and myself settled in on a nice farm in nearby Rio Linda, I was sitting in the dilapidated trailer I rented (Deaken's enclosure was nicer by far than the rattletrap trailer I was in, but wild animal owners live wherever their animals can live; we don't get to choose) looking out the window and daydreaming. Before I "came to" and realized what was going on, a tiny black and white kitten had wandered up to Deaken's pen, mewed at him and walked right in through the 2" chain link holes!

Every fiber of my being shrieked. I remembered Ralph Helfer's edict against allowing a serval to co-habit with other animals. I just knew that by the time I flew out the door of the trailer and keyed the security lock on Deke's pen, that little kitten would be a savory serval snack.

Nevertheless, I bolted out the door, grabbing the keys on the way. I opened the door to Deke's cage within six very fast heartbeats and then looked in… only to find the kitten standing on its tiny back legs with its front paws on Deaken's mid-chest, trying to get as close to his face as it could…

And Deaken was looking down, chirping, purring and licking the little guy!

I melted. Next thing I knew, Deaken was on his side with the kitten walking all over him.   Deke   was transfixed…twitterpated…utterly besotted. This was the best thing to come into his life since Zupreem!

I sat on Deke's den box for an hour, watching the two felines. Eventually the kitten curled into Deaken's chest and fell asleep on his front paws.

Never again was Deaken without a pet. Not once did he ever try to harm one.

I was utterly appalled that I had accepted an untruth, hook, line and sinker because a so-called animal expert had proclaimed servals among the "wild wild animals" that could never be trusted with other animals.

I had a parrot and a kitten who would beg to differ. And a fawn and a ferret to swear that what Ralph Helfer had claimed **was** true.

Deaken would eat a ferret, a deer, a possum, a snake, a rabbit. But he never offered to eat a cat, a kitten or a parrot.

In 1982 Deaken appeared in API's THE NINTH CRUSADE briefly, chasing grasshoppers in a field of dry grass. I was his "director."

Chapter Nine

Deaken Breaks His Leg (Again)

Not long after the API documentary was finished, I came home from work one day to find Deaken perched, breadbox style, atop his den box with his right rear leg dangling straight down over the side from his hip. The fracture was so severe I almost vomited, it upset me so.

I went in to see how he was doing. He was purring! His eyes looked clear and his pupils weren't dilated. He looked perfectly content! But he was warmer to the touch than I thought he should be, so I immediately called UC Davis and asked to speak to Dr. Ned Buyukmihci, who was one of API's premier veterinary advisors and a lifelong animal advocate.

I told Dr Ned what I could observe. He said that as long as Deaken was calm and unperturbed by the break, the best thing to do was just wait until morning because the swelling would subside by then and they could do more for him at that time. I agreed to wait until morning but confessed that even though Deaken appeared absolutely fine, *I* was a nervous wreck. "Just seeing it hanging there makes me half sick to my stomach."

He said, "Then don't look!"

Easy for him to say; harder for me to do, with my serval son's leg hanging there by what seemed to be just skin!

I called API and let them know I would be late to work the next day. I had Deaken at UC Davis by 8 a.m. then left for work.

The vet on staff looked him over, thought it over, then called me at work. He said, "We have two options. We can put it back the way it was, but it will remain just as susceptible to fracturing because the leg will be too stiff to bend when he jumps up and down from his den box. Or we can amputate and get rid of it altogether." I told him I had to think it over, thanked him, and hung up.

Then I bawled. My long quest to find a serval donor had failed. We were down to two lousy options. One would just invite more breaks and more pain. The other would break my heart because I wasn't able to find a better option.

In the end, I called back and said, "Amputate."

The vet said, "Good. If you had asked, I would have recommended that. It'll be so much easier on him. With the technology we have today, it will be a breeze. And because this is a teaching hospital, it'll just cost you $152.00. You can pick him up tomorrow."

"So soon?"

"Yes. Like I say, it'll be easier for him than it will for you. But… oh, wait! Tomorrow is Friday before a three-day weekend. But that's okay. I'll let you in tomorrow morning anyway, so he doesn't have to be away from you any longer than he needs to. Just stop by and knock on the door. And if you don't mind you can do rounds with me tomorrow morning before you take off—help me with the others patients. The students are going to be gone for the weekend by then."

"That would be great. I would love to do that. Thanks so much!"

"OK. See you tomorrow."

The next day before I took Deaken home I helped the vet care for an iguana, an owl, a coyote pup and several other critters.

As we worked, he told me about Deaken's surgery. "We have a state-of-the-art amputation blade that cauterizes as it cuts, so Deaken lost just 2 cc's of blood during the surgery. It went just great."

Deaken looked bright-eyed, "with it," and very chipper. When I got him home he slept half of the day and then went back to living life. The absent leg didn't slow him down a bit. He quickly adapted and could balance perfectly on his back leg. When I saw how well he did right away, I wondered why I had waited so long.

(A mother wants perfect solutions, not amputations. That's why.)

Within a week, Deaken was back to ambling in the cow fields, bobbing for frogs in the algae-covered pond and slapping at corn snakes.

Chapter Ten

Return to Washington

After four years in Sacramento, Deaken and I returned home to Eatonville, where we lived until Mom and Dad relocated to Spanaway (about 20 miles closer to Tacoma than Eatonville is). I worked at a pet store for a year or so and then took a job as an office manager of a continuing education school for real estate, insurance and securities agents.

In Eatonville, Deaken and I hung out a lot in the nearby forest. He'd lead the way (leash-less) and I'd follow. He almost always took me to an area where there were accessible low-lying bushes. I'd climb inside with him and lie there while he waited for small birds to fly in so he could try to catch them. He never caught one, but he came close a lot! I remember thinking it was a good thing he had me for a Mom-Cat because he would have starved as a predator! He just wasn't very good at nailing lunch on the wing… but then he had a good reason: he was a Tri-pawed!

We had two German Shepherds in Eatonville; one was the next door neighbor's but he was always over at our place with Ivanhoe, our dog. Deaken liked them both but they were forever having cross-cultural misunderstandings. A dog uses his forepaws for the exact opposite reason that a cat does. When a dog paws at you, he's asking you to play; when a cat paws at you, he's telling you to knock it off. So they were always a bit stymied by each other's communication skills. Still, when they weren't mis-communicating, they were peaceable and pleasant to each other.

When we moved to Spanaway, Deaken's pen was next to the house and visible from the long driveway. Mom and Dad never had any burglar problems, as a result, until Deaken and I moved back to California in 1989 so I could work in Hollywood. Within a month of Deaken's move, their house was burglarized!

It was while we were in Spanaway in 1986 that I reconnected with actor DeForest Kelley and his wife Caroyn after a 20 year absence. I went to a STAR TREK convention in Spokane and was flabbergasted to learn that they remembered me and had always wondered "what happened to the little girl that wrote so well." They invited me to reestablish contact and gave me their address so I could stay in touch. A lot of our subsequent communication was about "darling Deaken."

One day Mom told me she had called an appliance repairman but that she had to go into town. She asked if I would let him in when he arrived. I said sure.

When the doorbell rang, I found him standing there and invited him in. Immediately, Deaken lowered his head and began growling, then lowered his body and began slowly advancing on him. I had never seen him behave this way with anyone before! It made the hair on the back of my neck stand up.

I said, "Deaken! Whoa! What is the matter with you?"

Deaken halted and sat, but he continued to growl and glower at the fellow. It was then that I "got it." There was something about the guy that just didn't sit right with me. I kept a lot of distance between him and me and was happy when he finally left. To this day I don't know if he was a sexual predator or just a hunter. Whatever he was, Deaken had his number from the get-go. He never reacted in quite that way to anyone else again.

But Dad came home one night, plastered and in a belligerent mood, and Deaken took offense. Dad took offense at Deaken's offense and kicked at him. I yelled at Dad and pushed Deaken away. I know Deaken would have taken him on had I not done that. Deaken was my protector and defender. He knew a rotten attitude when he saw it. That's when I had to watch him closest.

Another memory: Mom was forever telling me to get Deaken out of her garden. He seemed to have a way of knowing exactly which flowers to sit among to most effectively reveal his beauty. I was always slightly insulted that she considered her garden lovelier with Deaken absent from it than when he was in the middle of it. It was a matter of opinion and perspective. Some of my favorite pictures of Deaken were taken in Mom's Spanaway garden!

Chapter Eleven

Hooray for Hollywood!

In 1989 after being encouraged mightily by Carolyn and DeForest Kelley to "give Hollywood a try," I flew down to take a battery of tests at Paramount Pictures. Miraculously, I passed their typing test at a rate of 89 words per minute for five minutes with zero errors, so the HR lady told me I would have NO problem landing a job at De's studio. They had eleven new shows planned; landing on any of them wouldn't be a problem.

I dropped the Kelleys a note sharing the good news of the interview and test results. Not more than a week later a package arrived addressed to "D. Smith." It took me two days to inspect the package more closely. Mom (Dorothea) and Dad had taken a trip to Alaska, so I had assumed the package was for her. But when I investigated the package again, I spotted the return address: Sherman Oaks, California! We only knew one couple in Sherman Oaks: the Kelleys. So I put film in my camera, carried the package to Deaken and helped him open it. As soon as I got the wrapping paper off, he began to drool and roll on the box… so I thought, "Gracious! What's *in* there?! A bottle of bleach?" (Deaken and Sneakers LOVED the scent of bleach and reacted toward it as though it were catnip.)

Inside was a lined, African animal motif diaper bag, roomy enough for at least a 24 pack of baby diapers. Accompanying it was a note from Carolyn:

> "Dear Kris,
>
> We hope Deaken will enjoy having his very own travel bag to accommodate all his gear on his trip here. We saw this bag the other day and decided it was just made to be Deaken's luggage.
>
> "Sue sent us the tape of your PACIFIC OUTDOORS show [a program on which I had been interviewed during my stint as an animal welfare activist at API]. We thought you came across just great, very un-self-conscious camera-wise. Are

you sure you don't want to be an actress?

"I can't remember if I ever told you that we enjoyed the tapes you sent us long ago, with your stand-up routine. Very good! And the shots of Deaken are terrific. Thanks even tho' it's late.

"Between you and me, want to tell you that De called __________ at Paramount [in HR] and gave you a boost – but told her, truthfully, that you had no knowledge of the call. Maybe it will help…De says hello and don't forget the chin tickles for dear Deaken. 'Bye – love, Carolyn."

I contacted Peter Rasmussen (of the ELSA WILD ANIMAL APPEAL), a southern California gentleman I had met during my time with API, to tell him I was looking for a place for Deaken to stay temporarily in his neck of the woods while I landed a job and found an amenable landlord. He quickly said, "I know the perfect place. Let me give them a call and see if they'll welcome Deaken for a while."

Not long after, he told me the owner of the sanctuary had agreed and that Deaken would be well-cared-for and welcome there. Then he told me which sanctuary it was: actress Tippi Hedren's Shamala Preserve (the ROAR Foundation) in Acton. He said Tippi would be calling me to be sure all of my papers were in order and then I would be free and clear to navigate.

So I met Tippi for the first time over the phone. She sounded (and turned out to be) fabulous. Shambala was heaven on earth for captive wild animals. She had spent several fortunes making sure it was before finally turning it into a non-profit organization.

So we packed up again, this time heading for Hollywood.

I knew getting Deaken back into California wouldn't be a problem (my record as a serval owner was unblemished in both states), but finding an amenable landlord would be the lynchpin to "happily ever after"… and I fretted about how many landlords would be willing to have a "wild animal" on their property? That was my chief worry, and the only remaining challenge--*or so I thought as I drove down!*--to staying in Hollywood successfully.

All the way to California (1200 miles), I let Deaken out of the car every two or three hours to stretch and relieve himself. Each time, when the rest stop was over and it was time to put him back into the car, he balked. He was very, very tired of being confined to a cat carrier for hours on end. He was used to having the complete run of the house.

So when we finally reached Shambala, I was as happy as I thought *he* would be. Finally, a place he could stay, with others like himself, for the first time in his life.

I thought he'd think he'd died and gone to heaven. I was wrong.

I had forgotten completely about the "Animal Sounds of Africa" record fiasco!

I had raised Deaken from infancy in a *human* environment. I had socialized and prepared him for a life with raucous, crazy, unpredictable HUMANS and their companion animals. I had always prided myself on having raised a completely HAPPY, completely NORMAL, remarkably un-neurotic "serval son." So when I opened the car door and put him out at Shambala on his leash, he took one sniff of the air, heard several lions roaring, and pulled me back to the car door, where he banged on it feverishly with his front paw, telling me in no uncertain terms to LET HIM GET BACK IN!

With a pang, I suddenly realized he probably had no idea he was a CAT, let alone a WILD cat!

I fell apart. I bawled. Talk about "separation anxiety" — I was afraid I had doomed my "baby boy" to a period of distress and anxiety second only to being set loose on the plains of Africa! Deaken knew by instinct that those lions were on the lookout for serval snacks. He had NO interest whatsoever in remaining within a hundred miles of this place.

When I saw Tippi approaching, I quickly dried my tears and greeted her with a smile. She said, "Hello, Kris. Welcome. And here's that darling little Deaken." He was, after all, the smallest cat on the place at that time. The others were lions, tigers, leopards, cougars and cheetahs! He looked like a "pocket panther" in comparison! I admitted, "Darling little Deaken is scared to death." She said, "Oh, we have a big enclosure for him, blocked off from sight of the other cats.

He'll settle in fine." Reassured, I said, "Okay."

Tippi took us to the enclosure. She was right. It was six times the size of the one I had brought down, and it was housed mostly inside a shed, with only a few feet of one end sticking out, where Deaken could get a glimpse of the other cats. Tippi said, "When he's all settled in, come up to the house and I'll get his Fish and Game paperwork from you and we'll chat a little bit."

I pulled out his rugs, toys, chairs, and other paraphernalia. I wanted to make the new enclosure as much like his old one as possible, so that HIS scents would reassure him that he was in the right place.

Tippi told me to feel free to come up as often as I wanted, days, nights, weekends, to reassure Deaken and to do as much for him as I could. She told me I could take him outside the compound on long walks. She told me I could stay there weekends if I so desired, so Deaken would know he was not abandoned. She reassured me he'd settle in quickly. I said, "I think he already has, pretty much. I put all his familiar stuff in the cage with him. He seems happy now."

Later that day, after I had gone, volunteer Leo Lobsenz went out to see the new addition. "Frankly, dear girl," he confessed to me later, "I nearly fell over laughing when I saw his over-stuffed chair, his rug, his mousey… Where were his television set and his refrigerator, I wondered!"

Mom and Dad drove me the rest of the way to LA, 35 miles distant. Sue Keenan, De's fan club president (with whom I'd be staying) greeted us. Later that evening, the phone rang. De and Carolyn were on the line, wanting to know how the trip went. I told them it went fine. Then Carolyn asked what Deaken thought of Shambala. I started to tell her of his FIRST reaction to hearing the lions roar:

"He slapped the car door, wanting to get the hell out of there as fast as we could!"

Carolyn burst into tears. I panicked and said, "Oh, but he's okay *now*, Carolyn! He's fine! Please don't worry!"

She apologized, "Oh, I'm sorry. I just could imagine, that poor sweet cat – scared to death!"

I said, "It made me cry, too, but he's okay now, I can assure you, or I wouldn't have left him there!" (As if I had any other choice!)

Chapter Twelve
Jobless in Hollywood

For the first fifteen months in Los Angeles, I stayed with DeForest Kelley's fan club president, Sue Keenan, while Deaken remained at Shambala. Upon my arrival in Hollywood, I called Paramount to let them know I had arrived safely, only to be told, OOPS! *None* of the eleven pilots had been picked up and the studio was completely staffed.

I was floored. I had told our hostesses, Tippi and Sue, that we would be staying with them perhaps 2-3 weeks, tops; maybe a little longer in Deke's case because I wasn't sure how quickly I would be able to find a landlord. Both quickly told me it was not a problem for us to stay longer.

Sue told me to register at the temp agencies in Hollywood that cater to the entertainment industry so I could get in the door that way with my good work ethic and reputation, so I did that.

But the work wasn't steady enough. There was no way I could look for a permanent place for us to live until I had a predictable, reliable income.

So whenever I wasn't working, and every weekend, I drove the 35 miles to Acton to be with Deaken and to reassure him that he hadn't been abandoned and that I would always be there for him. Every time I left he would cry piteously; every time I arrived, he would chirp copiously. We walked together a lot in the arroyo whenever we could.

During this time, De and Carolyn continued to console me, encourage me, and tell me that I was just one step away from having it made. Each time I got a job, even a long-term temporary one (lasting a few months) they would send a card or a plant, congratulating me and the new employer on our mutual good luck. Without their encouragement and help, I probably would not have stayed long enough for anything else to happen.

House hunting, Kelley style

As a temporary, I was gaining recognition and a good reputation and feeling that almost any time now I could consider myself "permanently employed" and start looking for an understanding, wildlife-loving landlord who would allow me to move in with an African serval cat!

As soon as I reported to the Kelleys that I was feeling "pretty secure" and that I'd be able to get a rental now and bring Deaken off the hill, they pitched in! They reviewed classified ads and called me often to report on places they had found that looked like good candidates. They suggested areas of the valley to search.

They even called a realtor friend and asked her to lend a hand.

Before long, another call came in from Carolyn. She just "had to" tell me a story: De had found a place where I could have Deaken! She told me that he had been driving around and had spotted this nice house not far from them. She continued, "So he stopped in there. The landlord happened to be there at the time, painting, so De stopped in. The landlord recognized De right away, and De told him he had a lady friend who needed to rent a home with a nice, high wall fence, and this place seemed to be a good candidate. So then De told him, 'The only problem is that she has a cat.' The fellow said, 'Oh, Mr. Kelley, a cat is fine; a cat is no problem.' So then De said, 'Well, it's a rather LARGE cat,' and the fellow joked to him, 'As long as it's no bigger than a LION, I have no problem with it,' and De said, 'Oh, no! It's no bigger than a lion!'

"So here's the address; you go on over there and introduce yourself and tell him that you're the girl De told him about."

She gave me the address and then I asked what the rental price was. She said, "$1350 a month."

I just about had a heart attack! I said, "Oh, Lord! That's WAY out of my league, Carolyn!"

She said, "It is?"

I said, "Heavens, yes."

"What do you want to spend?"

"Gosh… $550-600 a month, unless I find a co-renter."

That didn't end their search. Not at all. I'd be sitting at work and the phone would ring, and it would be Carolyn: "We drove around a little bit this afternoon, looking at rentals in your price range." (I was speechless!) "My hip is hurting me, so I couldn't get out of the car, but De knocked on a few doors and we have a few addresses we think you should look at!"

I could just imagine the looks on the faces of the people who had OPENED the doors after hearing De's knock! I wondered if any of them had passed out!

I confessed to the Kelleys that I felt I should wait until I had such an established record in the industry that there was NO WAY I would ever lose my job. De advised me, "The entertainment industry is probably the most insecure place there is to work. You'll never be able to count on it absolutely. You just have to proceed on faith. And we want you to get Deaken back home where he belongs."

So did I. So did I.

Chapter Thirteen
The Kelleys Meet Deaken

After seven months of waiting for me to get Deaken off the hill and into THEIR valley, without success, the Kelleys could wait no more. Carolyn called and said she and De would like to take a drive up to Shambala and meet Deaken. She asked if Sue and I would drive them there. I said, "Certainly!" She said, "Oh, good!"

We decided on a day. Then Carolyn said, "So, we'll see you here at the house at – oh, how about 9:30?" I said, "Sure. You'll have to give us directions."

She was astonished by that. "You have our address!" she exclaimed.

"Yes, I know," I said, "But neither of us have ever been by there."

She said, "You're joking!"

I said, "No, I'm not."

She couldn't believe that we hadn't driven by to "sneak a peek" at their home!

I assured her, "We're NOT voyeurs, Carolyn!" She said, "Oh!"

Excited and a bit rattled, Sue and I wondered which car to use. To us, my ten year old compact car didn't seem adequate for the occasion, while Sue was concerned that her larger, classic beauty might not have the gumption to get up the mountain.

Sue called Jackie Edwards and asked if we could use her new Hyundai for the occasion. Jackie was more than happy to oblige.

So, on the Big Day, Sue and I drove to the Kelley's house. We had no sooner pulled up than De and Carolyn came out the door, grinning, looking like two kids on their way to a candy store! Sue was in the driver's seat, and I figured De would join her in the front seat, and that Carolyn would join me in the back.

I was wrong.

De suggested that Carolyn ride "up front" with Sue, which she did. De climbed in the back with me. MY FAVORITE ACTOR in the rear seat with me, in a rather small vehicle. (This was only the second time in my life I had spent up-close-and-personal time with the Kelleys, so I was still feeling a bit twitter-pated and anxious about the prospect.)

We put on our seat belts and Sue started to back out of the driveway. De surprised me by grabbing my knee and grinning, "Hi, Kris! How ya doin'?!"

I darn near jumped out of my skin – and he could tell! I was SOOO embarrassed – and so was he!

I stuttered, "Aw… FINE! I guess! Thanks!"

Almost as soon as we got on the freeway, an inattentive driver came over into our lane without looking and just about wiped us out. Carolyn and I both saw the impending crash. Carolyn raised one leg to cushion the impact and I yelled, "Oh, God! Look out!"

Fortunately, Sue quickly got us out of harm's way, with only inches to spare! The driver continued on, blithely unaware that he had come *this close* to taking out one of the Big Three of STAR TREK!

No sooner had Sue avoided the collision, when De commended her, saying, "Great driving, Sue! Sure am glad we didn't dent Jackie's new car!"

Of course, the thought running through OUR minds (Sue's and mine) was, "Thank God the world wouldn't be reading about a VERY tragic accident on the highway!"

When we arrived at Shambala, we got out of the car and De noticed the back of my DeForest Kelley Hollywood Walk of Fame jacket, which I planned to wear at his upcoming star ceremony. De noticed the jacket – it was his first opportunity to see it since I had received it from a fellow Kelley fan. He queried humorously, "Who's that handsome fellow on your back?" I said, "Oh, some guy… I forget his name."

I directed everyone to remain very quiet outside Deaken's enclosure while I went inside to greet him, so they could see how we responded to each other without his being aware there would soon be other people entering his domain. I stepped inside the cage and greeted him, leaving the cage door open. He was sitting high atop his 5' tall den box, and when I hopped up to sit beside him, he greeted me with the customary mew and purrs and enthusiastic head rubs, then started watching the cage door, knowing that **something was up**. He continued to purr and head-rub, so I invited Carolyn in. (She was halfway in already: I thought that to delay her long-awaited meeting any longer might be detrimental to her health!) Carolyn came in, grinning ear to ear, and approached him. I told Deke, "This is Car'wyn, sweetness… the lady who sends you all those chin-tickles."

I'm sure Deaken didn't understand a word, but he instinctively understood the LOVE she was telegraphing to him and the fearlessness with which she approached him. He continued to purr and she came right up to him. He kissed her hand several times then rubbed his chin on the back of her fingers. She was in seventh heaven!

I jumped down from the den box and had Carolyn stand next to him so I could get a few photos of them together. After the photos, Deaken started looking outside the open door for other visitors and saw Sue and De standing there. A little growl arose in his throat, but nothing outrageous, and he continued to purr in between little growls.

Carolyn and I patted him and tickled him some more, and then Carolyn said, "De, come on in and meet him." Deaken let De come near, but hissed and mumbled, so De stepped back and said, "He's nervous, and I don't want to push him to do anything he doesn't want to do."

I said, "Let me carry him out of his own territory, so he won't be so protective of it." I wasn't sure that was the problem but I wanted to do something to reassure and placate Deaken. I leashed him and walked him outside the compound gates, to areas where we often "played," turning him loose in the elephant straw pile. He immediately settled in to roll and play in the stuff, which everyone enjoyed witnessing. He still wasn't amenable to having so many people near him all at once (one of whom was male, tall, and undoubtedly "a veterinarian with a big needle" to Deke's mind), so we just watched him play for a time from a relative distance.

After a while, I positioned everyone near Deaken and took a few group shots of the occasion. Deaken kept facing away from the camera, so occasionally I'd call, "De!" in a high-pitched, serval-like chirp, which was my way of getting his attention.

Well, it surprised me when DeForest stopped watching Deaken and looked in my direction every time I chirped, "De!" I laughed heartily and clarified, "When I chirp 'De', that's for Deaken. When I say (and here I assumed as masculine a voice as I could) 'De', that's YOUR cue."

De grinned and nodded – but forgot the next time I chirped, "De!" I laughed and he said, "OK, I'll try to forget that I'VE always been De, too!"

I said, "It should be easier for you than for a cat!" It wasn't.

I was delighted that Deaken was being civil and loving to the Kelley who most wanted to meet him "up close and purrsonal" – Carolyn – or this entire first visit would have been a fiasco. Deaken just wasn't into being a "celebrity" that day. But he did cope.

After the photo session in the straw pile, I put Deke away and said I'd take the gang on a trip through the compound. I directed Sue to drive to the first compound gate. "'I'll be the gatekeeper all the way through," I told her. "Any time we come to a gate, I'll jump out and open it."

Sue behaved and drove to the first gate – but as soon as I opened it, she drove through **and kept going**! I called out, "Hey! Wait for ME!" and ran after it and thumped on the trunk to get Sue to brake, so I could get back into the car.

I opened the back door to get in; De was grinning ear to ear and Sue said, "It was **his** idea. He **told** me to drive away and leave you wondering!" I threw him a feigned scowl. He loved it.

We proceeded to the next gate, and it happened again! De thought it was great sport.

They eventually got a complete tour – although I was quite out of breath from chasing the car down after every gate!

I told them I'd go get Deaken again and we could sit by the lake for a spell and relax. I walked to Deaken's cage and picked him up, then carried him back to the lake area.

When De saw me packing a 30 pound serval over my shoulder, he joked, "Is that how Deke gets his exercise?! No wonder he's having a tough time losing weight!"

I explained to De that Deaken didn't enjoy walking around in "lion country," as the king of beasts viewed servals as snacks, "and Deaken knows that."

Carolyn was completely enamored of Deke and stayed right near him while Sue and De walked around to view the lions, tigers, and cougars. She couldn't keep her eyes off him.

Shortly after we settled at the lake to take some photos of De with Deaken, Tippi came out to greet us. I introduced everyone, and they had a pleasant conversation. Tippi invited them back on a Shambala weekend (a weekend that would be open to the public). When the morning was over, I put Deaken away and we headed back to Los Angeles.

While Deaken was at Shambala and for several months afterward, I would always volunteer during Tippi's monthly Open House at the sanctuary. I would put Deaken on a leash and talk to Tippi's visitors about him. He was a small enough cat that they could sit down with him, so it was a cozy, comfortable event and always a lot of fun. The cover photo of this book was taken at Shambala by a visiting professional photographer. He gave me permission in perpetuity to use it in any way I see fit. Needless to say, I'm grateful!

One time Tippi was called away to appear at the opening of the Alfred Hitchcock exhibit at Universal Studios in Orlando, Florida so she called to ask if I was willing to ride herd on the sanctuary in her absence. She assured me that the animal caretakers would all be in place and that I would just be staying in her house to answer phones and act as an assistant. I was happy to oblige.

She said, "You can bring Deaken into the house the entire time I'm gone, too, and re-establish your relationship with him. It has been a long time since you spent significant family time together." I jumped at the opportunity.

I brought some books, blank paper, and a couple of videotapes to pass the evening hours. The lullabies of roaring lions were music to my ears and stirring to my soul.

One night I decided to put STAR TREK V (the Yosemite movie) on. Deaken was lying on a couch to the left of the TV about four or five feet from the screen. He appeared to be sound asleep so I was surprised when his head suddenly lifted off the couch to gaze at the TV screen.

What had drawn him there was Dr. McCoy's distinctive voice. And Dr. McCoy was dressed like the civilian Deaken knew, the one he had met just weeks earlier. The same man now stood before El Capitan on television, gazing at the cataract growling, "Playing' games with life."

Deaken stretched his nose toward the screen and sniffed, trying to catch De's scent. Nothing. So he sat up, stepped closer to the vision, and sniffed again.

By this time, Dr. McCoy was talking again. There was no doubt now: it was the same guy, scent or no scent.

Deaken didn't get it. He got down from the couch and came over closer to me. If that guy was back, on the other side of the glass, Deaken wanted to be closer to Mom-cat. He might have a needle, that guy. Most guys he met had 'me.

(Poor Deaken. If only he'd known that Dr. McCoy's needle was a hypo-spray...)

This was additional confirmation that Deaken was one smart cookie.

Chapter Fifteen

Kelleys to the Rescue!

After meeting Deaken and seeing the relationship he and I had–which was wonderful and trusting beyond belief–the Kelleys decided that he and I just HAD TO get back together under the same roof as soon as possible. I had by this time established a good reputation at the motion picture and television studio, but I did not by any means feel completely secure in it. It was again in a position as a "floater," and I didn't work steadily. I was getting great "reviews" from every person I worked for, though, and the Kelleys felt certain that I would have a job at that studio just as long as I wanted one.

They again began to look for places to rent. They found one in the newspaper in Encino, drove by it, and then called to tell me about it. I checked it out and fell instantly in love with it. It was PERFECT! I met with the landlord and, miracle of miracles, he even knew what a serval cat WAS, having seen one on a camera safari in Africa a few years previously. The landlord was happy to allow me to have Deaken there! I was on Cloud 9.

I had located a roommate – at the time living in Pennsylvania, but planning to move to the San Fernando Valley — and proceeded to let Fish and Game and the City Animal Regulation Department know the address and the other particulars, so they could inspect the area and okay the permits for Deaken.

It was only a matter of a few weeks, now, I thought…

Two days before the move-in fees and security deposit were due, my friend in Pennsylvania called to back out on the deal, saying she couldn't leave her mother, who was in failing health. I was BEYOND devastated. If I didn't get those fees to the landlord right away, not only would I lose my earnest deposit, I'd have to start all over again, from scratch, with permits and landlords.

I called the Kelleys from work, nearly in tears, and told them what had happened. They were easily as upset by the news as I was.

Then Carolyn said, "Kris, will you let us help?"

I said, "Oh, Carolyn, I can't. I can't get this place without a roommate. The monthly rent is $925 plus utilities. There is NO WAY I can afford it by myself."

She said, "Suppose a little fairy helps with the rent."

I said, "No way. Never. Thanks, but I could never live with myself if I did that."

She said, "OK, then, let us loan you the money for the move-in fees and the security deposit. You can pay us back whenever you can."

I repeated, "I can't afford that place by myself. I HAVE TO find a roommate."

She said, "You will. Now, you get that house and worry about a roommate later. It won't take long."

De got on the phone and said, "Get that house. Don't worry about it."

I moaned, "This is scaring the s— out of me." I had never spoken in "colorful metaphors" like that to them, ever.

He said, "I know it is – but do it anyway."

Carolyn got on the phone with me again and said, "De will get in the car right now and go get a certified check for the security deposit and the move in fees. What's your new landlord's address? I'll have him drive it over to him right now for you.”

I gave her the landlord’s address and then I started to cry. “Oh, Carolyn! You guys are so good to me! I’m crying!”

She said, “So am I! See you later!”

I hung up the phone and called the landlord’s wife to tell her that someone would be coming by to deliver the move-in fees and the security deposit. She was happy.

Then I felt obliged to forewarn her, “Uh, don’t faint when he gets there.”

She asked, “Why would I faint?”

“Well… did you ever watch the original STAR TREK?”

Hesitantly, she replied “Yes.”

“Well, the fellow who’s bringing the money is DeForest Kelley.”

"Which one was he?"

"Dr. McCoy."

She said, "Oh, my God!"

"He'll be by real soon."

She swallowed and said, "OK."

Later, she told me that she felt great trepidation waiting for De. She was under the impression that HE would be as irascible and quick tempered as McCoy was in his tiffs with Spock. Then she said, "But, Kris, when he walked in the door, he was just the sweetest, gentlest man I have ever met! And do you know what? He is your **biggest fan**! He says you are going to be famous some day!"

So, the place was MINE, at long last. On December 22nd of 1990, I moved in. I was certain that it would be a matter of days before my "serval son" would join me there. I couldn't wait!

But there was a glitch.

Although the inspections for Deke's facility had been made and approved, and the permits had been issued and were tacked on the facility door, the Fish and Game inspector hadn't been by for the "final" inspection. I called two or three times, but did not receive a call back.

Finally, I called and said I'd HOLD until someone could speak to me and let me know how soon I could expect the final inspection. A lady came on after a while and reported that the final inspection wouldn't take place for another "six weeks or so."

I just about flipped. I begged, I cajoled, I told the long, long story of how long Deaken had already been away at Shambala, waiting to re-join me. It fell on deaf ears.

Deflated, dejected, and utterly beaten, I hung up and cried.

I finally recovered and called the Kelleys, who had told me to call them the moment Deaken got home with me. I told them the sad story, and De again offered his help; he said he would call Sacramento for me.

I said, "Thanks, De, but I don't think even you can perform a miracle with a state agency. You can't fight City Hall. If what I told them didn't work, nothing will." De consoled me with, "Well, I know it's hard to wait, but six weeks is certainly better than six months." I agreed.

Then I hung up and cried again.

In early January, Desert Storm broke out. The newspapers reported that, depending on the length of the war, gas rationing might become necessary. I was living 35 miles away from Shambala! "If we get gas rationing," I told the Kelleys, "Deaken may as well be in SIBERIA! We'll only be rationed enough gas to get to work and back."

A day or so later, a Sacramento-based Fish and Game agent called me and said, "With Desert Storm underway, you'd better get up to Shambala right away and bring your cat home. I'll take the responsibility for any flack you get when our inspector finally gets there."

I thanked her, and Deaken was underneath my new roof within four hours.

I will never know for sure if De made the phone call to Fish and Game, but it is not outside the realm of possibility that he DID "fight City Hall" and win yet another battle for Deke and me. I suspect this, because not long after Deke came home, I got a very nice letter from Fish and Game apologizing for any inconvenience or extra trauma their delays may have caused me or my loved ones.

How many times does a state agency write such a letter?

A day later, the Kelleys arrived for a tour of my new digs and to see how well (and how immediately) Deaken had settled in. I found a roommate, and all was family bliss again.

Who's Visiting Deaken Today?

Encino, for all its citified pretenses, is still prime stomping grounds for possums, raccoons, skunks, squirrels, snakes, coyotes and other mammalian, reptilian and avian San Fernando residents. I know this because, from time to time, curious creatures would visit our back yard and carry on, scurry away, or meet their Maker depending on Deaken's decision as to whether they'd make better playmates than menu items.

During a single week in May, the week preceding Mother's Day that year, Deaken polished off an entire litter of baby possums, one per night, leaving only their naked rat-like tales, tiny feet and snouts as evidence of his predations. On the morning after Mother's Day, I found the mother's remains in his pen. I wondered how the heck a fully-grown female possum could get into such a small gauge chain-link enclosure; never did figure it out. But I was happy to know that he had eaten them in the right order: babies first, then the mom. That way the babies didn't starve, at least!

A few months later just after sunset, I smelled the inimitable reek of beleaguered skunk in the back yard and went out to see what had caused the animal to fire his putrid mess into the atmosphere. You guessed it: Deaken sat there, miserable, pawing at his nose and face, half-sick from the full barrage. It had become patently obvious to him that **this** black and white "kitty" **did not** want to play!

Holding my breath as best I could, I carried Deaken into the house and put him in the tub with as much tomato juice and sauce as I had on hand and scrubbed him until he felt better. It took days for the residual stench to leave his fur and the back yard, but it was the last time he tangled with a skunk.

Not long after we moved to Encino and settled in, I adopted a young kitten. I named her Popcorn because of her whimsical habit of "popping" straight up from the floor as she played. Later—after she settled down—she became Poppy.

Like the kitten in Sacramento before her, Poppy immediately and without hesitation "adopted" the big spotted cat as her Papa Kitty. Deaken was in seventh heaven. He would lie prostrate on the ground, indoors and out, and allow her every indignity she could come up with: biting his throat, nursing on his non-functional teats, burying her nose in his gigantic ears.

By the time Poppy grew into a gangly half-grown terrorist, she was something to be reckoned with in the back yard. Because Deaken was a tri-pawed, she knew just what she had to do to bowl him over—and he knew that **she** knew. So he would begin hopping into the middle of the yard, watching (with a serval smirk on his face) for her ambush. He knew it would come, and Poppy never disappointed him.

She would launch herself from the side of the house or from under a bush, hit him in the rear end where his absent leg was, and watch him fall. Not that he **had to** fall; he was delighted to fall and willingly fell over and then waited for her to rush in and "finish him off." She would bite and kick and he would purr and lick.

It was one of the most heartwarming displays of mutual affection I have ever seen. I wish I had a video camera back then. I'd probably be a gazillion ire today.

Of course, it wasn't just animals who visited Deaken in his back yard. Famous people visited him there, too, among them Carolyn and DeForest Kelley, AC and Martha Lyles, Richard Arnold of Paramount, a well-known animal expert, and exotic Veterinarian to the stars, Chris Cauble.

Two of the visits were particularly note-worthy:

When Dr. Chris Cauble and the (so-called) animal expert stopped by, it was to film an episode of the animal expert's TV show. Dr. Cauble called me one day when it was time for Deaken's annual checkup and asked me if I would allow the man and his film crew to document the visit and the check up. I said, "Sure!" He said, "Instead of you being my assistant after we put Deaken out, I would like ______(name obscured to protect the guilty!) to be my assistant. You can stand right by, out of camera shot, but I would like him to do the assistant work."

I said, "Works for me. Fine."

On the day of the shoot I had to pretend there was no camera or film crew in attendance and welcome Dr. Cauble and said animal expert into my home. I did that; then, held Deaken while Dr. Cauble administered the knock-out shot. Deaken obligingly went down.

They quickly rearranged the scene and put the animal expert in my place, with a stethoscope clutching his neck. Dr. Cauble told him to monitor Deaken's heart rate while he checked out my sleeping beauty and took a vial of blood. He nodded.

All well and good--except that I was suddenly horrified to discover that the ear pieces of the stethoscope were still clasped around Mr. Animal Expert's neck instead of in his ears where they needed to be to monitor Deaken! *They had been working on my cat without monitoring his heart for more than three minutes.*

During the next break, I informed them that they might want to actually install the stethoscope earpieces into the fellow's ears. Everyone laughed.

They had to do a little re-taping to cover the oversight. And I berated myself for not noticing the issue at the outset. Instead, I had simply assumed that this man was carefully monitoring Deaken's heartbeat, and that assumption could have resulted in fatal consequences.

It was a good lesson. I never forgot it. State and federal inspectors and TV show talking heads are not always the sharpest tools in the shed so please don't rely on them to take good care of your animals.

Chapter Seventeen

Deaken Bites Mom (again)

All her life, for some unfathomable reason, my mother had rotten luck with animals. Geese bit her as a youngster, bats dive bombed her as an adult, and Deaken bit her—twice! By contrast, I have been involved with just about every kind of animal, from salamander to snake to serval to simian, from leopard gecko to leopard, from lamb to lion, from goose to goat, and never run afoul of them. I have a natural affinity for them.

Mom was amazed that birds and butterflies landed on me when I was a toddler. I don't remember ever NOT loving animals to the core of my being. I think that's what probably signals to them that I'm okay and safe to be around. I have worked with chimps, bears, camels, elephants, tigers and more. The result is always the same: a sense of kinship and peace.

Looking back, I'm astounded and beyond grateful to Mom that she allowed me to have and love animals, given her own history with them!

One evening quite late Mom went into the garage to move clothes from the washer to the dryer. Her recollection of what happened next: "I didn't know Deaken was in there. He was probably asleep. I don't know if I stepped backward onto him or if he came to me from somewhere, but all of a sudden he bit me—hard—above the ankle on my leg."

Startled, Mom jumped and pulled away. Her reaction caused a huge chunk of meat to be pulled out of her leg as

Deaken unlocked his jaws, backed up, and moved away.

Mom came into the house and said, "Kris?" I said, "Yeah?" She said, "Deaken just bit me." I looked down. Her grey sweatpants were soaked through with blood.

I said, "Oh, Mom! Crap! What happened?"

She said, "I must have startled or stepped on him. I didn't know he was in there."

I took a look at the gash. It was ghastly. She said, "It's nothing."

I said, "No, it's something! We have to get this looked at."

I quickly called Tippi—she would know what to do in this situation. Tippi said, "Take her to urgent care but don't let them cover the wound tightly or stitch it up. It has to have air; it has to breathe or it may become infected."

I asked, "Are there any legalities to navigate? Do I have to report this anywhere else?"

She said, "No. Deaken is legal and unless your mom plans to sue, you're fine."

I told Mom what Tippi said. Mom responded, "Sue?! Sue who? My grandson? It wasn't his fault!"

I called Urgent Care because by now it was about ten minutes to ten in the evening and they were supposed to close at ten.

I told the doctor who answered the phone, "My Mom just got bit by a big cat."

He thought **big domestic cat** and responded, "Oh, that shouldn't be a problem. Just clean it real well. Do you have Beta dine or a triple antibiotic on hand?"

I clarified, "Yes, I do, but you don't understand—this is a significant bite. It took a thumb-sized chunk of meat out of her leg. She really needs to be looked at by YOU!"

He said, "Wow! OK. We'll stay open. Bring her right in."

When we got to the clinic and he surveyed the wound, he was amazed. "What kind of cat did you say bit her?"

"My grandson," Mom replied. "He's a serval. I stepped on him. It was entirely my fault."

Mom was cool as a cucumber.

The doctor smiled and said, "You're not from around here, are you?"

She said, "No. Why do you ask?"

He laughed, "Most of the women in this town would be hysterical or in shock if this happened to them."

She said, "I'm a farm girl. This is nothing."

He looked and it again and disagreed: "Hardly."

I felt guilty, guilty, guilty. Deaken should have been sequestered in his pen, not sleeping in the garage. It was a valuable lesson. Thankfully, it happened to Mom and not to an Encino housewife or superstar. We lived to love another day, unscathed by scandal.

Chapter Eighteen

Natural History Magazine Blessings

In 1991 or 1992 I learned that an animal researcher named Aadje Geertsema was studying servals in their natural habitats in Kenya. Looking a little deeper, I found an address for her and wrote to her about

Deaken, wondering how closely Deaken mirrored untamed relatives in his sire's home country. Aadje sent me a copy of the Natural History Magazine to which she had contributed an article about her discoveries in serval country.

What I read and saw in those pages had me in tears. Deaken was 100% serval. Although born in captivity and tamed from birth, he still had every characteristic and behavior of the wild servals I read about in those pages. In fact, I even entertained the notion (still do!) that the wild servals Aadje was studying were actually his direct kin. They looked so much alike, it was astonishing. (Seriously! Just google "serval images" online to see how very different servals look from each other. The photos in **Natural History** looked as much like Deaken as any other photos I have ever seen, before or since, with just minor differences.)

The way Aadje described their gait, hunting techniques, habits, and everything else just confirmed what I had always hoped for: that I had raised a serval without somehow changing who he was… without messing with his head or his habits.

It was extraordinary confirmation that I had done a lot of things right, even though I was a greenhorn, to all intents and purposes, when it came to actually raising a serval from infancy to adulthood.

Chapter Nineteen

Landlord Bails, New Home Search

My landlord, pushed over the brink emotionally and financially by the Northridge quake and by the expense of repairing his two rental properties plus his own place, mentioned to me that he and his wife were considering selling out and moving to Florida. The news panicked me. He wanted OUT. I recalled how long it had taken to find a landlord willing to let me have Deaken. Still, with the landlord's pressing concerns and incessant fear, I could well understand his need, so it seemed to me a dead certainty that, before too long, I'd be searching for new digs, the difficulty of such a search be damned.

I considered moving back to Washington. Mom and I both vetoed that idea, with

Mom saying, "Much as I'd love to have you move back here, you'd be insane to move back solely for a cat that's about to expire anyway. That just doesn't make good sense at all."

So it came as a big relief when the landlord reconsidered and told me I could stay for at least another six months. It would buy enough time for a sane, rational approach to the next housing option – and who knew, perhaps Deaken wouldn't even be a factor in six months, since he was now 15 and sliding downhill health-wise. Searching for a housing situation sans Deaken would be a picnic compared to looking for a place for him and me.

Mom and Dad arrived on Halloween Day while I was at work and called in to let me know they were at my home.

On November 30th, the axe fell. The landlord sent a move-out notice, giving us 90 days to find other digs, as he had made the decision to move out of

California and re-locate to Florida. I was beside myself with worry. I was enormously glad that Mom and Dad were in Southern California for the winter and could scout for options while I worked.

Carolyn and De called often to tell us of places they'd heard of, and to try to keep my panic at a manageable level. Deaken was the obstacle. And I wasn't about to have Deaken euthanized out of expediency. No way. I'd give up my career and everything I had going for me in Southern California if it came to THAT. The commitment I'd made to Deaken the first time I held him in my arms, at five hours old, was inviolate.

In December, Emese Fisher, my guardian angel Realtor, kicked around the idea that rather than locating a rental, we should go for the purchase of a house or condo. Dad was for it. "You'd OWN the place, you wouldn't be pouring money down a rat hole."

The decision made, I let the Kelleys know of the new direction. Carolyn wanted to know how I would come up with the down payment! I said, "Dad and Mom said they can help with most of it. I just have to be sure and get it back to them by summer."

"Why?"

"Well… they're both retired and on a limited income."

She said, "We could loan you the money. No interest. Up to ten years to pay!"

I balked. They insisted, saying "Now you can relax a little bit and find the perfect home for you and Deaken with much less strain and trouble for everyone."

On March 13th 1995 we moved my belongings to the new condo and began unpacking with our remaining, albeit lagging, energy. I'd just recently had Deaken's necessary permits transferred to the new location, but kept quiet about him to the condo association and to my new neighbors. I'd had enough crises for the time being; I certainly intended to avoid any others that were attributable to sharing my life with a geriatric, three-legged, rapidly failing "wild animal."

Chapter Twenty

The Condo Floods, Deaken Discovered

One eventful evening just two months after Deke and I moved into the new condo, we were hanging out in the living room when it began to rain hard—INDOORS!   The fellow in the condo above me had not replaced the plumbing that we had all been advised to replace. I shrieked, grabbed Deaken and carried him into the bedroom, then heard frantic knocking on my door.

By now the entire hallway ceiling was being inundated with water; it was running into the light fixtures and pouring onto the carpet at my feet. Shutting the bedroom door to keep Deaken from following me back into the living room, I ducked through the deluge and threw open the door. The occupant from upstairs stood there in a long white shirt and undershorts (thank God), but no trousers. I took a brief look downward to confirm what I thought I had seen (sure enough, the guy had no pants on!), then back at his face.

He said, "Kris, I'm so sorry. I'm doing absolutely everything I can."

I said, "That's fine. Goodbye!" I tried to close the door to get back to Deaken, but he pushed it back open. "I want you to know I've called the Fire Department. They'll be here as soon as they can."

"Fine. Okay. Let me close the door now."

He went back upstairs.

I raced to the garage, slammed Deaken's carrier into the back of the car, and raced back to the house to get Deaken so I could remove him before the authorities arrived. I didn't know if I'd be required to leave and get a hotel, or what, but I did know that NO ONE at the condo complex, if I could help it, would know that Deaken was in residence there.

I got back to the front door just as Pants-less Neighbor descended the staircase in my direction again. Swinging around to confront him, I said, "Yes, what is it?"

He said, "I just want to say again how sorry I am."

"It's fine. Really. No biggy. Go back upstairs and put some pants on, will you?"

Almost as if realizing his condition for the first time, he said, "Okay." He headed back upstairs two steps at a time.

I figured he'd probably be back—or the Fire Squad would arrive—any second, so I quickly grabbed Deaken and carried him around to the garage, placing him into his carrier, then ran back to the condo just as the Fire Department arrived.

We didn't have to leave, as it turned out, but I did spend the remaining eight hours until daybreak squeezing out as much water from the carpet and other flooring spaces as I could.

Of course, I had to get three estimates to satisfy the insurance company and the resident handyman had to take a look, too. The problem was that the resident handyman was so pro-active and friendly that he knocked on the door and barreled past me into the back bedroom almost before I could say "Hello!" -- only to find Deaken lying on the bed staring at him.

I whimpered, "Oops…"

He said, "What is that?"

"A geriatric 3-legged serval. I have all the required permits. I just…" Words failed me. I was busted, with a capital B.

The fellow said, "Do not, under any circumstances, tell anyone else about this animal here at the complex. No one. If you need any repairs, you call me. Here's my number. Got that?"

I wanted to hug him but because we were in my bedroom I figured it wasn't the best of ideas, since I hardly knew him. I said, "God bless you. God bless you, sir."

He said, "I'm happy to help. What's your cat's name?"

There are guardian angels on this planet. You just don't know they're there till you need them.

Chapter Twenty One

Deaken's Final Days, the Kelleys' Helping Ways

About a year later in the middle of the night Deaken suffered either a stroke or a spinal injury and became unable to right himself or to stand. His obvious distress roused me from sleep. I called his veterinarian, Dr. Chris Cauble, right away. He asked me about his vital signs; I reported them.

I told him Deaken was very unhappy and upset by his inability to function and I thought it was coming close to the time when he should be put down. The vet agreed, and said he'd come out the next morning to evaluate the situation and see if euthanasia was the only proper solution.

I dropped off a note letting the Kelleys know what was happening. They called right away after reading it to console me. Carolyn started off with, "We're so sorry to hear about dear Deaken." De pretty much took over from there, because Carolyn and I both began sniffling and wiping our noses.

De told me what a happy, wonderful, long life Deaken had with me. "I understand how difficult it is to make a decision like this one – we had to do it with Fancy – but don't feel guilty about it."

I sniffled, "I don't feel guilty. It's for HIM. I want him with me forever – but he will be, whether he's here physically or not. I just don't want him to suffer or to be unhappy."

De asked, "Are you planning to cremate him?"

"Probably. I think so. Yes."

"That's best."

Carolyn said, "Our thoughts are with you and our hearts go out to you. Give dear Deaken a chin-tickle for us, will you?"

I said, "I sure will. You bet. I love you. Thanks."

After the veterinarian evaluated Deaken's condition and recommended a waiting period to see if he would recover without risky and costly medical intervention, I called Mom and Dad to let them know what was happening. Mom said, "You just take good care of my grandson and yourself."

The next few weeks were a roller coaster of emotions – elated at each minuscule (or imagined) improvement that Deaken showed, dejection and fear with each set-back. I tried to keep my reports positive, but not wildly hopeful – and I tried to keep them humorous, as difficult as that was.

I regaled the Kelleys with reports of midnight butt-dips and bedding changes. At one point, when I could see Deaken wasn't making the comeback we hoped for, I told Carolyn that I almost wished Deaken was a little more miserable than he was, "because it's going to be hard to put him down when he doesn't seem to be suffering. But of course, he's not suffering ONLY because he's on pain killers."

She agreed. "It's a tough call, but it's the right one, Kris. He doesn't have the quality of life now that thrills him, or one that makes your life easy or happy, being constantly concerned about his comfort and hygiene. It's time. He has had a wonderful life up until very recently. A wonderful life. You don't want it to end in frustration for him."

I sighed and agreed. "No, I don't."

The next day, I called Dr. Cauble and made arrangements to have Deaken euthanized on Cauble's next available date, September 11th. I wrote it on my calendar and then went into the bedroom to snuggle and caress the love of my life, knowing I'd just sentenced him to death. He kissed my wet face and purred.

Carolyn called shortly thereafter, while I was still sniffling. She asked, "De wants to know if you want him to put out some more newspapers for Deaken or do you have enough?"

I said sadly, "No… I won't need any more, thanks. I've made arrangements to have him put to sleep on the 11th. He's not happy in his present situation and it doesn't look as though he's going to walk again."

Carolyn said, "Oh, I'm so sorry, Kris. You're a loving mom-cat to do that for him. I know it's tough, but it's absolutely the right decision."

I sniffled, "I know, or I wouldn't be doing it, believe me! It's really a terrible decision to have to make."

On September 8th, De was in Huntsville, Alabama at the 30th Anniversary STAR TREK Weekend. Carolyn stayed home, and of course I was spending my last weekend with Deaken. She called in the afternoon to see how I was doing. When she heard my subdued voice, she asked, "Are you crying?"

I said, "Oh – off and on!"

Carolyn asked, "Is Deaken having a bad day?"

 "No, he's having a WONDERFUL day. We've had a lot of fun today – he's been purring and kissing me and hugging me with his front paws. It's just that whenever someone calls to see how I am or to tell me to hug him for them on Wednesday – as Dad did just a few minutes ago — I tend to fall apart."

I laughed through the tears and Carolyn said, "Oh, my!" sharing my anguish.

Then she said, "De thought of something. We discussed it before he left and again this morning on the phone. We'd like to pay for Deaken's vet bill and his cremation services."

I said, "Oh, Carolyn, that's not necessary, but thank you anyway."

She said, "I know it isn't, but we'd like to do something, and this is what we've decided to do."

I protested, "You've already done so much for me."

She said, "This is our contribution to your commitment to Deaken. We want to do it, and I want you to send me the bills as soon as it's all over and we'll send you a check for the amount."

I was sniffling again and said, "All right. Thank you."

Dr. Cauble gave Deaken a sedative to relax him completely prior to the final injection. His assistant, Gigi Grossman, and I were at Deaken's side. Deaken was propped mostly in my arms. I rubbed his belly with great aplomb and tickled him the way he loved. He reached over and gave me a little purr and a kiss but his eyes were dull. He was ready to call it a day; I could tell.

Tears were leaking out of my eyes, but I was handling my emotions very well, in a sort of transcendent manner, to keep from transferring my internal anguish to Deaken.

Dr. Cauble said, "Well, if this is any consolation, I heard from a spiritual friend that the ease with which we leave this life is the ease with which we enter the next phase of our existence in the afterlife. If that's true, you are giving Deaken the best sendoff I have ever witnessed. He's going to be very happy very soon."

I said, "I hope so. He deserves it – don't you, baby boy? He's the best."

Then he said, "Okay, let's do it." He took Deaken's back leg and injected the lethal solution.

Within seconds, Deaken relaxed completely, sighed, and passed over to wherever serval souls go.

For some strange reason, I felt elated. I had managed to handle my emotions in such a way in Deaken's last moments of life that I was certain he had felt only my love and joy regarding the life we'd shared together. I knew he had felt no anxiety or fear or concern at all. I almost couldn't wait for the veterinarian to leave so I could call the Kelleys and report the good news.

I had Deaken cremated and kept his ashes in a box in my bedroom, but I couldn't mention his name aloud within earshot of Poppy. She was completely inconsolable.

She kept mewing and looking, mewing and looking for him. After several days of this, I asked her, "Poppy, what do you want?!" exasperated and—as God is my witness—she hopped up on the nightstand, reached up the wall and tapped a photo of Deaken with her left paw, then jumped down and lay down where they used to sleep together.

It was too much, just too much for me.

I went out and adopted two domestic kittens and brought them home. Poppy didn't like them much, but at least it shut her up and gave her something else to think about until they won her over. I would not have survived anguish deeper than my own—and I sensed that hers was in some way deeper.

Chapter Twenty Two

Our Hearts

<u>DO</u> Go On...

About two months after Deaken's death, I was standing in my living room near the front door facing the radio console. I wasn't thinking about Deaken; my mind was on something else entirely.

Suddenly, metaphysically, I sensed a cone-shaped "opening" from the ceiling to the floor next to me, about three feet wide at ceiling height and perhaps a foot wide across at floor level. The opening was filled with light and warmth I could <u>feel</u>. I sensed Deaken's spirit within it. Immediately, "My Heart Will Go On," sung by Celine Dion, came on the radio.

The virtual cone remained in place for at least 20 seconds, then slowly began to dissolve. Again, I couldn't see it with my physical eyes but I sensed it with my spiritual eyes and heart. I knew it carried Deaken's essence. There has never been any doubt.

Some Christian denominations don't believe animals go to heaven. I believe heaven would be hell without them. Those of us who love some animals as much as we love some family members cannot imagine a heaven without a Rainbow Bridge. I certainly can't.

Since Deke's passing I have been visited in my dreams at least twice a year by him. He is well, he is whole, he is at the perfect age (just past the "gangly teenage" stage in cat years)… and he always rushes to greet me as if he has missed me as much as I miss him.

I look forward to the days when we'll be together again, never to part.

SERVAL VIDEOS AND SOUNDS AVAILABLE ONLINE

http://www.bing.com/videos/watch/video/serval-making-serval-sounds-grunts-yips-squeaks/28ce749786b8b208290528ce749786b8b2082905-712222835867?q=serval+sounds&FROM=LKVR5>1=LKVR5&FORM=LKVR

http://www.youtube.com/watch?v=Fowu72-dKvM

http://www.youtube.com/watch?v=BZOkSNz6qSY&NR=1&feature=fvwp

http://www.youtube.com/watch?v=gN7pSWMsJ4A&feature=related

http://www.youtube.com/watch?v=xvJs4D0nR8Q&feature=related

http://www.youtube.com/watch?v=IrimMUsYHxY

http://www.youtube.com/watch?v=RH9FsuQQOIQ&feature=fvwrel

SERVALS IN THE WILD (info)

http://www.wildwatch.com/living_library/mammals-2/serval

http://en.wikipedia.org/wiki/Serval

http://www.pictures-of-cats.org/serval.html#Introduction

http://www.pictures-of-cats.org/serval-threats-and-conservation.html

Additional Wild Cat Information

Shambala/The Roar Foundation
http://www.shambala.org/

http://www.youtube.com/watch?v=52iOqBNcjcw

http://www.youtube.com/watch?v=Yu6bPcUohWY&feature=related

If you have enjoyed this book
please consider the following titles by
the same author…

**Available at
YellowBalloonPublications.com
and Amazon.com:**

Floating Around Hollywood. Always
amusing (and often downright hilarious)
collection of reminiscences by Kris
Smith spotlighting her adventures as a
"floating secretary" (temporary) in Tinsel
Town.

A.C. Lyles, legendary producer

and goodwill ambassador to the entertainment industry at Paramount Pictures, writes, "Kris Smith's entertainment industry career reads like a sitcom."

DeForest Kelley's back cover comment is, "A fast-paced book, full of laughter, written with comedic skill. It's a delightful read."

Let No Day Dawn That the Animals Cannot Share.

Foreword by DeForest Kelley
Art by Emese Dian

A mostly-serious collection of Smith's animal" pros-e-try" which will clutch passionately at your heart and spirit. The book spotlights humankind's deeply-rooted emotional, ethical and spiritual bonds to the animal kingdom, wild and domestic, and then identifies areas in which we have fallen painfully (and dangerously) short regarding our stewardship of scores of precious and irreplaceable fellow creatures. (Get out a box of tissues for this one.)

DeForest Kelley Up Close and Personal: A Harvest of Memories from the Fan Who Knew Him Best

The actor best-remembered as a science fiction icon is recaptured in word and deed in this affectionate and affecting personal memoir.

Kris writes, "We need honorable role models who do not disappoint once the camera lens turns away. De was my friend, but he was also my hero - one of very few heroes whose durability was sorely tested yet found to be utterly reliable. I wrote this book to show how deeply De influenced my life - and to remind you, his fans and friends, how seamlessly and comfortably he fit into yours. For the millions of fans who did not have the chance to meet De up close and personal, this is your gateway...Enter, heartstrings attached!"

If you know DeForest Kelley solely through his 50-year acting career in motion pictures and television, this book will become a treasured keepsake. For true fans of all ages.

The Enduring Legacy of DeForest Kelley: Actor, Healer, Friend (e-book, by request only!)

DeForest Kelley's former personal assistant Kris M Smith has compiled the memories and reminiscences of fans and friends whose lives were blessed and changed forever by the career or kindness of the late actor who portrayed Dr. Leonard McCoy in the original Star

Trek series. All who contributed to the tome have realized the immense impact that the iconic "Bones" has had on their lives and careers. Smith reveals that Kelley's enduring legacy includes fans who continue to boldly go where few have gone before, making a difference every step of the way."

Settle for Best: Satisfy the Winner You Were Born to Be

Settle for Best lists the common mindsets and actions of renowned philanthropist millionaires from the early 20th century and encourages readers to develop and rely on the skills and mindsets that successful people still use to win big, no matter what shape the economy is in. Written for start-up entrepreneurs and anyone else anyone in search of the "keys to the kingdom" in whatever realm you travel, SETTLE FOR BEST will encourage, inspire and light a fire under you if you truly want to build the life and legacy your heart most desires.

Become Shamelessly YOU: How to Stop Hiding in Plain Sight

What's keeping you stuck in F.E.A.R. (False Evidence Appearing Real) Mode?

What is it that you don't want anyone else to know about you, so you're hunkered down, hiding in plain sight?

You weren't born to blend in. You were born to stand out. Why aren't you?

False modesty?

Your upbringing and conditioning?

Something in your present or past that makes you feel "unworthy" of leaving a positive lasting legacy?

Why are you letting your mindset, missteps or mistakes keep you from feeling fantastic about yourself? The fewer secrets you keep, the better off you'll be.

In this helpful, proactive guide, we'll visit the secret shames that so many people carry around with them. Once they're exposed, it will be easier to respect and embrace your potential, so you can step out of the shadows and into the spotlight where your unique contributions can help change the world.

WOMB MAN: HOW I SURVIVED GROWING UP IN A BOOBY-TRAPPED WORLD

When I was 32, I did something that made my father immensely proud. Spontaneously, he proclaimed **"That's my boy!"**

Immediately, Dad realized what he had said and shot a panicked look sideways at me, his mouth agape, eyes wide with horror.

Equally shocked, catching my breath, but somehow relieved, I responded, "It's all right, Dad." I had to repeat "*It's all right*!" because he looked so undone, so unspeakably **sorry**.

But it really was all right because, for the first time in my life, I felt recognized for who I was: a **remarkable man**.

We never spoke of it again. But I began to wonder why it had taken 32 years for my father to "get" me. *Or had it? Did he know something I didn't? And if he did, why was he keeping it a secret?*

I will never know for sure. So, the questions remain…

Was I born **intersex** and surgically altered as an infant to meet gender norms (the default 'solution' in the mid 50's for ambiguously-gendered babies, then called hermaphrodites); am I naturally **transgender—a man housed in a female body**; or did "nurture" (the way my parents reared me) have something to do with it?

There are a lot of individuals like me out there who don't fit gender norms. Many of them feel they need to hide who they truly are just to exist without being scolded as strange or feared as foreign. You probably know several of them;

they just don't trust you enough (yet) to tell you.

Something needs to change. I hope my own story helps that happen.

About the Author: Kris M. Smith is a professional copywriter and author with a sincere devotion to all of creation.

A Pacific Northwest native, Kris's freelance writing career was launched by actor DeForest Kelley more than fifty years ago. It was Kelley and his wife Carolyn who encouraged Kris to try Hollywood on for size.

Kris served as Mr. Kelley's personal assistant and caregiver during the final months of his life and presented heartfelt sentiments about him at Paramount Studios' memorial service for him in 1999.

In Hollywood, Kris served as an administrative assistant and secretarial floater to writers, producers and—later—information technology professionals at various studios. Most of Kris's Hollywood career was spent at Warner Bros. Studios.

See and hear interviews with Kris at yellowballoonpublications.com and krisandkritters.com.

Email Kris at: kris@wordwhisperer.net

NOTES

NOTES